The Children's Edda

Volume 1

by Dan Coultas

illustrated by Lørna Marshall

First edition

Published 2022 by Dan Coultas & Lørna Marshall

Copyright © 2022 Dan Coultas & Lørna Marshall

All artwork by Lørna Marshall, Anglesdottir Arts

@anglesdottirarts

Edited by Debi Gregory

ISBN: 9798364908186

Contents

Introduction

This book is about the Gods and Goddesses that live in the magical realm of Asgard. These stories were told long ago by people including the Norse, Danes and Anglo-Saxons. They spent the long cold winters around fires in their wooden longhouses discussing the mythology of the north.

We know these stories because they were written down around 1000 years ago in two collections, known as the Poetic Edda and the Prose Edda.

The people who originally told these stories believed that they were true, and that the Gods and Goddesses in them were real. There are still people who believe this today, and they are known as Heathens. Most of these Heathens communicate with the Gods and Goddesses through prayers and rituals and believe that they can affect our lives.

This doesn't mean that they don't believe in science. Stories like the creation of the universe are a way of understanding the big bang and evolution. It's normal to believe in the Gods and Goddesses and believe in science.

This is the first book of a series that will re-tell some of the best-known stories about the Gods and Goddesses of Asgard, as well as the giants, animals and humans they meet.

I hope you enjoy these stories and learning about the Gods and Goddesses of Asgard as much as I have enjoyed interpreting them for you.

How the World Began

A very long time ago, before our world was made, even before the Gods and Goddesses existed, there were only two realms.

One of these worlds was called Muspelheim. Muspelheim was very hot. So hot in fact, that all the rocks had melted into lava, and everything was on fire.

The other world was called Niflheim. Niflheim was very cold. So cold in fact, that all the water had turned to ice, and everything was frozen.

Between these two realms was a huge empty space called Ginungagap, where there was nothing at all. No water, no air, not even any light.

Muspelheim the fire realm, and Niflheim the ice realm grew into the empty space from either side, and after a very long time, the ice and the fire met in the middle and joined together to make a mighty giant called Ymir.

Ymir was very big and strong, but he wasn't very nice.

Ymir had a cow called Audhumla. He milked Audhumla for cheese to eat and milk to drink, as there was no other food because nothing else had been created yet. As time went by other giants grew out of the sweat from Ymir's armpits! That is how the giants were created.

The cow Audhumla licked at the ice to get water to drink. She licked and licked for years and years and eventually, slowly but surely, she licked away so much that a frozen God was released from the ice where he had been trapped! His name was Buri, and he was the first of the Aesir family of Gods.

Once he was out of the ice Buri had a son, who he called Bor. Bor grew up, and once he was old enough he married a beautiful giantess called Bestla, and they had three sons of their own.

These children were called Odin, Vili and Ve. That is how the Gods were created.

Odin, Vili and Ve grew up to be very strong. Once they were big and strong enough they hunted down the big bad giant Ymir and killed him. They took his skull and turned it into the sky, then took his body and turned it into the land.

Finally, they took his blood and turned it into the sea. That is how all the worlds were created, including Asgard where the Gods live, and Midgard where we live.

Now that they had made Midgard it was time for the Gods to create people to live there. They found an elm tree and they turned it into the first woman, who they called Embla. Then they found an ash tree, and they turned it into the first man, who they called Ask.

The three Gods each gave Ask and Embla a gift. Odin gave them the breath of life. Vili gave them the ability to think. Ve gave them the gift of speech. That is how people were created.

Now you know how the world began.

How Thor got his Hammer

Have you ever wondered how Thor got his mighty hammer, Mjolnir? Or maybe how Odin got his spear, Gungnir, or Freyr his magnificent golden boar, Gullinbusti? Well, that's a long story…

One morning after another lively party in Aegir's Hall, Thor woke up. He opened his eyes, stretched his arms, let out a big yawn and turned over to look at his beautiful wife, Sif, who, incidentally, was very proud of her beautiful blonde hair. He went to kiss her, but there was a problem; her beautiful golden blonde hair was gone, and Thor's kiss landed on a bald head.

As soon as he had recovered from waking up to this shock, Thor got very angry, and he knew exactly who he was angry with. "Loki!" Thor shouted. "What have you done with my wife's beautiful hair?"

"I don't know what you mean!" said Loki, with a sly grin on his face. Thor did not believe him for one second. He picked Loki up and pinned him against the wall.

"I can keep you up against the wall all day Loki until you tell me what you have done." said Thor.

Loki didn't feel like spending all day pinned up against the wall, so he told Thor what he had done.

"Okay, okay." He said. "I pulled it all out in the night, whilst you were both sleeping, I thought it would be funny."

"Well, it's not funny at all." said an increasingly angry Thor. "Will it grow back?"

"Umm, no," said Loki. "I'm afraid it won't."

Thor roared in anger and pushed Loki hard into the wall.

"Wait!" squealed Loki as Thor squashed him. "It won't grow back, but I can replace it, with even better hair, made of real gold, that will join to her head just like real hair."

Thor loosened his grip a little.

"I will give you one week to get this golden hair and put it on Sif's head," he grumbled, "and if you don't, you won't want to come back to Asgard ever again!"

So off Loki went to find some magical golden hair that would attach itself onto Sif's head just like real hair. Surely that couldn't be too difficult?

Now, everyone knows that the greatest treasures are made by the dwarves, so Loki went to Svartalfheim, the land of the dwarves, to find the most skilled dwarven craftsmen he knew; three brothers known as the Sons of Ivaldi. Dwarves are very skilled, so their work is very expensive, and as Loki had no way to pay them, he knew he would have to use all his skill and cunning to get them to make the hair he needed.

"Are you the Sons of Ivaldi, the most skilled of all dwarven craftsmen?" Asked Loki.

"You know we are!" said one of three brothers, who looked so alike that even clever Loki could not tell them apart.

"Well, you see, I've been travelling around, and when I travel around I hear things," said Loki with a sly grin on his face, "and I heard the brothers Brokk and Eitri say that they are far better craftsmen than you. They said they are going to make three gifts for the Gods of Asgard that will be better than any three things you can make, so that everyone in the nine worlds will know that they are the greatest craftsmen."

Now, none of this was true of course. Loki had never even met Brokk and Eitri, but he knew that dwarves are very proud, and wouldn't be able to resist such a challenge.

"Nonsense!" said a different one of the sons, or was it the same one? Loki couldn't tell. "We will make the Gods three gifts that will be far greater than anything those two amateurs can make!"

"You'll need to bring the gifts to Asgard one month from today." said Loki, "oh and one more thing, I almost forgot. One of the treasures you make needs to be golden hair, beautiful golden hair that will attach itself to a head just like real hair."

"We can do that." said one of the sons, and off Loki went to find Brokk and Eitri, pleased that the first part of his plan had worked perfectly.

He walked for many miles across Svartalfheim until he came to the forge where Brokk and Eitri lived.

"I have come with a message for you from the sons of Ivaldi!" Loki proclaimed. "They say that you are no craftsmen at all! They say you are amateurs, and to prove how much better than you they are, they have challenged you to make three treasures for the Gods of Asgard. They say that the treasures you make will be nothing compared to what they can make, and everyone will know who is the best!"

Brokk frowned. He was the cleverer of the two, but not as skilled at craftsmanship, so he worked the bellows for his brother Eitri.

"I know who you are, Loki Lauffryson, and I do not trust you!' He said. 'I smell your mischief! What does this challenge have to do with you?"

"Why nothing at all!" said Loki, looking as innocent as he could. "I was simply passing this way, and they asked me to give you the message, nothing more."

Brokk was not convinced.

"We will accept this challenge Loki," he said, "but as I do not trust you I will need you to accept a bet. If we win this contest against the Sons of Ivaldi, and the Gods decide that our treasures are better, then you must give us your head!"

Loki did not like the sound of losing his head one bit. After all, he had become quite attached to it. But he needed Brokk and Eitri to make three treasures to be judged by the Gods, as otherwise his whole plan would fail.

"Fine," said Loki reluctantly, "if you win the contest, my head will be yours." And off he went to work out how he was going to make sure that there was no way that could happen.

His plan was still on track, this was just a little set back, right? A little, potentially head losing, set back. Loki was sure he was clever enough to work it out. Sif would get new hair, the Gods would get their treasures and Loki wouldn't get beaten up by Thor. And as long as he could stop Brokk and Eitri winning the contest, he would not even lose his head. What could possibly go wrong?

Loki sat and thought about how he was going to stop Brokk and Eitri from winning the contest without them knowing it was him. He decided that the best thing to do would be to disguise himself and cause some mischief. Loki could transform his shape to whatever he liked, so he decided to transform himself into a horsefly, that could fly and bite.

Eitri had decided on the first treasure he was going to make. He told his brother Brokk that because these treasures had to be perfect, he had to pump the bellows just right. If he went too fast or too slow, the temperature in the forge would change, and the treasure would be ruined.

So Brokk started to pump the bellows up and down, with a perfect steady rhythm.

"That's great," said Eitri, "keep that up and I will make a treasure for the All Father, Odin."

Eitri took a lump of metal and started to heat it in the forge, then beat it on his anvil. Brokk pumped the bellows up and down. Slowly but surely the lump of metal was transforming into a magical golden ring. The brothers were nearly finished when a fly swooped down and bit Brokk hard on the neck. It really hurt, but Brokk knew he had to keep pumping, so he ignored it.

The ring was finished, and it was perfect. Eitri was very happy with it.

"Well done Brokk," he said, "do the same for the next two and we will definitely win this contest, and get Loki's head!"

Loki scowled; he would have to try harder.

Brokk started to pump the bellows again. Eitri took another lump of metal and started to heat it in the forge.

"This time I shall make a gift for Freyr," he said.

All was going well, until the fly came back and bit Brokk right on the nose.

"Ouch!" shouted Brokk, but he kept his hands on the bellows, and kept pumping. The fly bit him again, but he ignored it and kept pumping the bellows, up and down, until Eitri was finished.

"Look Brokk," he said, "I have made a golden boar for Freyr. Just one more treasure to make and victory will be ours. Soon we will have Loki's head!"

Loki was very angry. He really did not want to lose his head. This time he would have to do everything he could to ruin this last treasure.

Brokk started to pump the bellows again, and Eitri started to craft a treasure for Thor.

"This will be my greatest creation," said Brokk, "the one that will definitely win us this contest."

This time Loki didn't hold back. He swooped down and bit Brokk all over his face, his arms, and his chest. Brokk tried his very best to keep pumping steadily but the fly just would not stop biting him. He took his hand off the bellows for just a second and swatted the fly away. Loki only just managed to get out of the way, but he hoped he had done enough to ruin this treasure.

Eitri came out of the forge, holding the treasure he had made for Thor.

"What happened brother?" He asked Brokk. "You stopped pumping and now this hammer that I have made for Thor has a short handle. Still, even though it is not perfect, I think it will be good enough to win."

The day of the judging came. Odin, Freyr and Thor sat on thrones, and the Sons of Ivaldi brought in the treasures they had made for them. First of all, they approached Odin.

"All Father, we are honoured to present you with this." said one of the Sons and presented Odin with a spear. Odin looked pleased.

"This is a fine-looking spear," said Odin approvingly.

"This spear is named Gungnir," said the Son of Ivaldi, "it is the greatest of spears. It will always fly straight and never miss."

Next, they approached Freyr, and presented him with a small leather pouch.

"This may just look like a pouch," said one of the Sons, "but inside it is a ship, the fastest ship there is, and it is big enough to fit all of the Gods and Goddesses inside. When you are not using it, you can fold it up like a piece of cloth and carry it in this pouch."

'Excellent!' said Freyr. "This will be very useful indeed."

Finally, the Sons approached Thor. Reached into a bag, one of them pulled out what looked like a golden wig.

"This may look like a wig," said one of the Sons, "but when your wife places it upon her head, it will attach itself just like real hair and shine like gold."

"Let us put it to the test!" said Thor. "Sif, my love, this dwarf has a gift for you." Sif had been wearing a headscarf ever since her hair was stolen by Loki. She walked up to the Sons of Ivaldi, and slowly took off the headscarf. There was a gasp from all the Gods and Goddesses as they saw Sif's bald head. She knelt down, and the dwarf placed the golden hair upon her head.

Straight away it attached itself to her head. She stood up and gave her new hair a swish. It looked just like real hair, but shone like gold.

"Excellent!" said Thor, and turned to Loki, "looks like I won't be beating you up after all!" He said, and slapped Loki on the back. Loki smiled; he was sure that

these treasures would be better than those that Eitri had made.

The Gods thanked the Sons of Ivaldi for their gifts. Now Brokk and Eitri approached them with their gifts. Firstly, they presented Odin with a golden ring.

"This ring is call Draupnir," said Brokk, "and every nine nights another nine gold rings will drop from it, so you will never run out of gold."

"A fine gift indeed!" Odin placed the ring upon his arm.

"Not as fine as the spear Gungnir though." Pointed out Loki, but everyone ignored him.

Next, they approached Freyr, and presented him with a shining golden boar.

"This is Gullinbusti," said Brokk, "he can run across land or water faster than any horse, and he can fight with the strength of fifty warriors when you ride him into battle."

Freyr was very pleased.

"It's good," said Loki, "but remember how great your folding ship is Freyr." Once again nobody paid much attention to what Loki had to say.

Finally, they approached Thor.

"This is the final and greatest gift," said Brokk, holding out a hammer to Thor, who took hold of the handle.

"The handle is a bit short, isn't it?" asked Thor, not looking too impressed, which cheered Loki up a lot.

"Well, yes," said Brokk, "but this is not just any old hammer. This is Mjolnir, the hammer of the Gods. When you throw it, it will hit its target, and then come straight back to you."

Thor's face began to light up, and Loki began to scowl.

"It will break whatever you hit with it," Brokk continued, "but it will never get broken."

"Enough talking," said Thor, with a big grin on his face, "let's see if what you say is true!" And with that he swung the hammer above his head and threw it as hard as he could. It went straight through the wall with a bang. Then there were three more bangs as it went straight through whatever was on the other side of the wall. After a few seconds the hammer came whizzing back though the hole in the wall, and straight into Thor's hand.

Thor let out a roar of delight.

"This is the greatest thing ever!" shouted Thor. "This competition is over!"

A look of panic came onto Loki's face.

"But…but…what about your wife's beautiful hair?" He stuttered.

Thor was throwing the hammer up in the air and catching it, grinning from ear to ear.

"What? Oh, yes, Sif's hair is very nice," he said, not taking his eyes off the hammer.

"But…but…Odin? Freyr?" Pleaded Loki. "What about your spear? What about your ship?"

"Those are both wonderful treasures," said Odin, "but with this hammer Thor can protect Asgard from all of our enemies."

"I agree," said Freyr, "my ship is brilliant, but the hammer will benefit us all, and keep us safe. We all agree that the hammer is the best treasure, so Brokk and Eitri are clearly the winners."

"Excellent," said Brokk, "hand over your head Loki!"

Loki glanced at the door to see if he could escape, but there was no way out. He would have to think very, very quickly if he was going to keep his head. Luckily for Loki, he is a quick thinker.

"Of course," he said slyly, "you can take my head, we had an agreement after all."

Brokk drew his knife and stepped towards Loki.

"But," Loki said, stopping Brokk in his tracks, "you cannot take any of my neck, that wasn't in the agreement."

"That is ridiculous!" said Brokk. "I cannot take your head without cutting your neck!"

"Well, that's not really my problem is it?" said Loki, who was now very, very pleased with how clever he was. Brokk turned to Odin.

"All Father," he pleaded, "what do you think about all this?"

Odin leaned forward.

"It is true that your deal with Loki did not include his neck,' he said, 'so you have no right to cut it."

Brokk scowled; Loki grinned.

"But…" said Odin, wiping the smile off Loki's face, "you do own his head, so maybe there is something that you would like to do to it without removing it?"

Brokk thought for a moment. He whispered to Eitri, who nodded.

"I will sew his lips together." said Brokk, "so he can't spread any more lies."

"Seems fair to me!" said Odin. Freyr and Thor nodded. Loki tried to make a run for it, but Thor grabbed him and pinned him down, whilst Brokk went to go and find a needle and thread.

So, there you have it. Now you know the story of how Thor got his hammer, Sif got her new hair, Odin got his spear Gungnir and golden ring Draupnir, Freyr got his golden boar and his folding ship, and Loki managed to keep his head.

And if you were wondering, eventually the stitches dropped out, and Loki was back to his mischievous ways, just the way we like him.

How Asgard got its Wall

It was the first day of winter and all the Gods and Goddesses decided that Asgard, their home, needed a wall to protect it from the giants but they didn't know anyone that could build one that would be big and strong enough. The next day, somebody new arrived at Asgard. A builder, with a big horse called Svadilfari . The builder said that he could build the wall in three seasons. But as payment, he asked for the sun, the moon and for the Goddess Freyja to be his wife. "Go and wait outside," said Odin, and the man went to wait outside so the Gods could decide what to do.

"He is asking for too much," said Thor, "we should send him away, and maybe I should use my hammer to make sure he stays away!"

"I don't want to marry him," said Freyja. "So, I think it is a very bad idea."

"You won't have to!" said Loki.

"What do you mean?" Asked the Gods and Goddesses, who were a bit confused.

"There is no way he can finish the wall in time but, just in case, we should tell him we won't give him three seasons to build the wall, we will just give him one," said Loki. "If he hasn't finished the wall by the first day of spring, we will chase him away and pay him nothing." The Gods and Goddesses thought that Loki was very clever and agreed to the plan.

They told the builder and he agreed too, as long as his horse could help him to move the stones that he would need to build the wall. So, the builder started to build the wall. Each day he would go away to the mountains to get the stones and his horse would help him to bring the stones back to Asgard. He would spend the night building the wall and then set off again the next day for more stones.

The wall got bigger and bigger, and stronger and stronger, and the Gods started to worry that the builder might finish it in time and they would have to give him the sun and the moon and Freyja would have to be his wife. The last day of winter came and the wall was nearly finished. All the other Gods were very angry with Loki for making them agree to the plan. "I don't want to marry that builder!" said a very angry Freyja.

"And what about the sun and the moon?" Asked Idunna. "We can't afford to lose those!"

"Don't worry," said Loki. "If we can stop his horse from helping him, he won't be able to finish the wall in time and we won't have to pay him."

"How can we do that?" Asked Odin.

"Don't worry," said Loki. "I think I know a way". Loki had magical powers which meant he could change shape into anything he wanted. He turned himself into a mare, the prettiest mare that anyone had ever seen. When Svadilfari the horse saw Loki as a mare, he fell in love. Loki ran away and Svadilfari followed. The builder called him back but he was in love with Loki the mare and nothing the builder could do would bring him back.

The builder had to go to the mountain by himself but without his horse he could only bring back one stone. One stone was not enough to finish the wall and as the next day was the first day of spring, he didn't finish the wall in time.

So, the Gods had a wall that they could finish off themselves and the builder had to leave without the sun, the moon or with Freyja as his wife. Loki's plan had worked. But where was Loki? Nobody had seen him since he ran off with Svadilfari. Svadilfari had loved Loki the mare very much and after one year away, Loki came back.

But he was not alone. He had a little foal following him. Not a normal foal either. This foal had eight legs and would grow up to be the biggest and fastest horse in all the worlds. His name was Sleipnir and he would be Odin's very own horse.

Now you know how Odin got his horse, and Asgard got its wall.

Thor's Wedding

One day when Thor woke up, something very, very bad had happened. His hammer, Mjolnir, that he used to protect the Gods and all the people on the earth from giants and monsters, had gone missing.

Thor was very worried, but he knew that when bad things happened, it meant either Loki had done it or Loki would know how to fix it (or sometimes both!). So off he went to find Loki and tell him what had happened.

"Oh dear," said Loki. "That is very bad news, I haven't taken it but I will go and find out who has." So, Loki went to see Freyja and borrowed her magical eagle cape so that he could fly. He flew off from Asgard, to search across all the worlds for Thor's hammer, until he came to the place where the giants lived.

There he met a giant called Thrym, who had a bag that looked like it might have something hammer shaped in it. Loki asked him what was in the bag. "It is Thor's hammer!" said Thrym, who seemed very pleased with himself. "And I will only give it back if Freyja will become my wife!"

"Oh dear," said Loki and off he went back to Asgard to give the Gods and Goddesses the bad news.

None of the Gods or Goddesses were very happy but Freyja was very angry indeed. "I will not marry that giant!" She shouted.

Thor was very angry too. "I will go there and beat them up and take my hammer back!" He said.

"You can't," said Loki calmly. "Without your hammer you won't be able to beat them."

The Gods and Goddesses all tried to think of a plan to get the hammer back without Freyja having to marry the giant Thrym.

Finally, Loki, who loved tricks, had an idea. "I've got it!" He said. "Thrym has never actually seen Freyja and we all know that giants don't have very good eyesight. So, if Thor dresses up and pretends to be Freyja, he will be able to get close enough to take the hammer back."

"That sounds like a much better plan than me actually marrying him." said Freyja and all the Gods and Goddesses agreed. Well, almost all of them…

 "I'm not putting on a dress and pretending to be Freyja!" said a very grumpy Thor. "You'll all laugh at me".

"It is the best plan we have," said Odin, who had been listening quietly. "So, you are just going to have to do it if you want your hammer back." So, Freyja went to find her prettiest dress and all

the Goddesses helped to braid Thor's hair, put make-up on his face and make him smell like sweet summer flowers.

But even after all of this, Thor still looked like a big grumpy man with a big red beard, that he would not shave off. So they put a veil over his face and hoped Thrym would not notice. Loki, who could use magic to change shape, turned himself into a pretty young maiden to be Thor's flower girl, then Thor dressed as Freyja and Loki the flower girl went off to the land of the giants for a wedding.

When they got there, Thrym had put out a huge wedding feast to celebrate. This cheered up Thor, who had been very grumpy, and had not said a word to Loki the whole way there.

Thor sat down and started eating. He ate two whole cows, four pigs, a sheep and two trays of vegetables, as well as all the little snacks and cakes that were meant for all of the guests. When he finished, he let out a very loud burp!

"Gosh," said Thrym. "I never thought the beautiful Freyja would be able to eat so much!" Loki had to think quickly to make sure Thrym did not work out that it was actually Thor in the dress and not Freyja.

"The beautiful Freyja was so excited when she found out that you wanted to marry her, that she could not eat, she has not eaten a single thing since she found out and that is why she is so hungry now." Loki told Thrym, who seemed happy enough with that answer.

Next the servants bought out drinks for all the guests. Thor, still dressed as Freyja, grabbed the first jug, which was meant for a whole table, and gulped down the whole thing in one go. He did this again and again, until he had drunk ten whole jugs. This time he let out an even louder burp! "Gosh," said Thrym. "I had no idea the beautiful Freyja would be able to drink so much!" Once again Loki had to think quickly.

"The journey here from Asgard was very long and the beautiful Freyja refused to drink anything at all on the way because she was so excited to marry you," he said. "And that is why she is so thirsty now." Once again, Thrym seemed happy with this answer.

"Let me look at the face of my beautiful bride." said Thrym and before Loki the flower girl could stop him, he lifted up the veil that was covering Thor's face. He was expecting to see a beautiful face but instead he saw a pair of eyes that were red and burning like fire.

"Gosh!" said Thrym. "I never expected the beautiful Freyja to have such angry looking eyes!" Once more Loki had the answer.

"She is not angry," said Loki. "But since she found out that she was going to be marrying you, she has been so excited that she has not been able to sleep and that is why her beautiful eyes are so red and sore." Once again, Thrym seemed happy with this answer.

"Enough!" said Thrym, standing up so everyone could hear him. "It is time for the beautiful Freyja and I to be married. Bring out Thor's hammer, so that we can use it to bless our marriage!"

One of the other giants came out with the hammer and placed it in Thor's lap. I'm sure you can guess what happened next. As Thrym lifted the veil to kiss his bride, Thor grabbed the hammer and hit Thrym with it as hard as he could, sending him flying across the room.

"Nobody steals my hammer!" shouted Thor, who ran around the room, hitting all of the giants with his hammer. Once he was sure that they would know never to try it again, he took off the dress, Loki turned back into his usual self and the two of them went back to Asgard to tell the Gods and Goddesses what a good job they had done.

Thor made them all promise to never mention again that he had worn a wedding dress and pretended to be Freyja but if you listen very carefully on a quiet night, you can still hear them giggling about how grumpy it had made him to this day.

Idunna's Apples

One day Odin, Thor and Loki were exploring. They had been walking all day and they were getting very hungry. They decided to stop and cook the food they had brought with them.

Thor collected as much wood as he could in his big, strong arms.

Loki lit the fire using his magic.

Odin put the food on his spear so they could roast it over the fire.

They waited for an hour, but when they checked on the food it was still cold. Thor grumbled then went to go and get more wood for the fire.

This time he built an even bigger fire, and Loki made sure it was burning extra hot to make sure this time the food would cook. They waited another hour, but when they took the food off Odin's spear, it was still cold. It still hadn't cooked at all and the Gods could not understand why.

"I can't wait any longer!" shouted a very angry Thor.

At that moment Odin noticed that there was a very big eagle watching them from the tree next to their fire.

"What are you looking at?" Odin asked the eagle.

"I am looking at your fire," said the eagle, "and I see it is not cooking your food. If you share some of your food with me, I will fan the flames with my wings, so it will burn hotter and the food will cook."

The Gods were not too happy about sharing their food, but felt they had no choice.

"Okay," said Loki, "we will share our food with you eagle, but you can only have the same amount as we each have, even though you are so big."

With that, the eagle swooped down and beat his wings. The fire flared up, and the food was cooked in no time at all. Odin took the food off his spear, but before the Gods could share it out, the giant eagle swooped down from the tree and grabbed almost all of the food.

The Gods were very angry. Loki tried to grab the food back. The eagle dropped the food, but he grabbed Loki, and flew up into the air!

The eagle flew for many miles with Loki in his claws. He flew across fields and lakes; he flew across mountains and he flew across the ocean until he came to a small iceberg floating in the middle of nowhere. He swooped down and put Loki on the iceberg. Loki shivered. He was cold and scared.

"What do you want from me?" Asked Loki. "I will do anything you want if you take me back to my friends."

"There is one thing you can do," said the eagle, "you can steal Idunna and her golden apples that keep the Gods young so that they can live forever. I would very much like to live forever, and my daughter Skadi is very lonely, so Idunna can be her friend."

"The Gods will be very angry," said Loki, "but if you take me back I will get you Idunna and her apples."

So, the eagle took Loki back and dropped him next to Odin and Thor, who had saved him some food. They all agreed that they should get back to Asgard before anything else bad happened.

The next day Loki went to visit Idunna at her orchard where she grew the golden apples.

"I am feeling old Idunna," said Loki, "may I have a golden apple so that I can be young again?"

"Of course, you can," said Idunna, and passed him an apple.

Loki ate the apple and immediately looked young again.

"I think they are," said Loki, "and I can show you."

Idunna didn't really trust Loki, but she had to be sure that there weren't any better apples. She followed Loki into the dark forest, with her golden apples in her basket so that they could compare them with the apples that Loki said were better.

They walked for a long time, and Idunna started to wonder if these apples even existed. Just as she was going to turn around and head back to her orchard, the eagle swooped down and grabbed her and her apples.

"I am not just an eagle," he said, "I am the giant Thjazi in eagle form, and now I will live forever!"

"Oh dear," said Loki. "Maybe the Gods won't notice that Idunna and her apples are gone, and everything will be fine."

The Gods did notice. Everything was not fine.

Without Idunna's golden apples to keep them young, they started to get old. Their hair was turning grey, their skin was getting wrinkled, and they were starting to feel tired and weak.

Thor knew that if something was wrong it either meant Loki had done it, or Loki could fix it. This time he had a suspicion that it might be both, so he went and found Loki and pinned him up against the wall.

"Where is Idunna? Where are her apples?" He shouted.

"I don't know what you are talking about," said Loki, "why do you think I would know?"

Odin always knew when Loki was lying.

"You do know," said Odin, "and if you don't tell us we will let Thor hit you with his hammer until you do."

Loki had been hit by Thor's hammer before. He had not enjoyed it very much. So, he told the Gods what had happened, and before Thor could hit him, he promised to get Idunna and her apples back.

"I will need your eagle cape Freyja," said Loki and she went to fetch it for him.

Loki put on the cape and flew off to find Thjazi's castle. He found Idunna and her apples in the tallest tower of the castle, and he perched on the window ledge. Idunna wasn't very happy to see him.

"What are you doing here Loki?" Asked Idunna. "I don't want to see you; this is all your fault."

"I'm here to save you," said Loki. "Just close your eyes, hold onto your apples, and I will get you home."

Loki used his magic powers to transform Idunna into a walnut. He took the walnut and flew off. Thjazi saw Loki escaping and turned himself back into an eagle to chase him.

They flew all the way back to Asgard. Loki flew as fast as he could, but Thjazi was even faster. Loki was nearly at Asgard's wall, but Thjazi was catching him up.

Luckily for Loki, the Gods and Goddesses had a plan. They had built a big pile of firewood in front of the walls. As soon as Loki had flown over it, Thor lit the fire. Thjazi was flying too fast and he could not slow down. He flew into the fire, which burnt off all his feathers. Without his feathers he could not fly over the wall into Asgard, and he fell down to the ground.

Loki gave Freyja her cape back and turned Idunna from a walnut back into her usual beautiful self. She gave golden apples to all the Gods and Goddesses so that they would be young and strong again. They all felt much better as soon as they had eaten them. Their wrinkles disappeared, and the colour came back to their hair. Idunna was very happy to be back, but she would never follow Loki into the dark forest again.